The World's First Drunk
With Counselor Talking Points

By Robert Villegas

The World's First Drunk
With Counselor Talking Points
By
Robert Villegas
© Copyright 2016 by Robert Villegas
Contact: rville9755@aol.com

ISBN 9781539406938

Published in the United States of America.

www.robertvillegas.com

Dedicated to My Father

Robert Regino

Table of Contents

Introduction

> "Is it the gods…who put in our hearts /
> This burning desire…or else / Does
> each man make of his own wild
> yearning a god?"
>
> > -   Virgil, The
> >   Aeneid

The ideas in this book provide a secular approach to addiction that is founded on real values that the individual identifies for himself. This departs from the traditional religious views that impose altruism as a prime value. According to the traditional view, your prime value should be other people and serving them – it should not be about you.

I wrote this book to help develop a new model for people trapped in the cycle of addiction. It is my view that the religious premises of the current Alcoholics Anonymous organization must be re-considered. As I made my journey through substance abuse, I had the opportunity to observe these premises and I judged them as defective because they didn't relate to my life and circumstances. As a consequence, I had to develop a different path that worked for me.

The ideas, and especially the ten-step secular program offered in this book, are based upon my own battle with addiction. I want to state clearly that I am not a professional working in the field of addiction; I am an individual who has dealt with addiction as part of my own private struggle. I do not hold myself out to be a counsellor, a psychologist, psychiatrist or a doctor of any kind specializing in the field. I am a person who dealt with these issues as part of my own private struggle. What I learned about myself and the issue of addiction is based upon my own experiences. I had to develop my own knowledge, my own intellectual tools and I do not hold these ideas out to be the final answer that will create a life-changing metamorphosis for my readers.
I offer these suggestions for your consideration as well as for the consideration of counsellors who are seeking new tools and a new understanding of addiction that does not provide the obligatory religious perspective. In fact, my perspective is secular – without religion – and I think that this perspective might provide some interesting

insights for counsellors mired in the repetition of old and unworkable faith-based ideas that have provided little in the way of understanding in the past. My approach is secular but also "cognitive". I focus on knowledge and the process needed for "changing one's mind" rather than for merely changing one's actions. I offer no miracles, no guarantees and no promises. I am merely suggesting that the key to addiction, as I have learned, is found in reason, the mind and changing what one thinks.

To put it bluntly, the religious approach to addiction is counter-productive and even harmful. Certainly, the advocates of the religious approach want to help alcoholics and their dedication and hard work should be appreciated. However, I think there is a better secular way. It is hoped that this approach will assist the reader in also beginning his own journey of understanding.

The World's First Drunk

This story is a fictional telling of the life of the Stone Age man who invented alcohol. Learn about the effects that alcohol had on this man's thinking processes, his social life, family life and financial life. This part of the book is intended as an object lesson on the harm and dangers of excessive alcohol consumption written by a person who grappled with these issues for years.

"Today was an incredible day! I feel great! Today I discovered something wonderful."

"You seem different. Your eyes seem different. Why are you smiling so strangely?" said Shela, my wife.

"I was out looking for grapes, like you told me. And just like I always do, I eat while I pick. Let me look at myself."

I ran to the water hole by our hut to see my reflection, to see if I looked different. I was smiling such a large smile that my face was contorted and red. But I felt pleasant. I enjoyed it. I continued my story to her.

 "So today, I was picking from the vines that grow low to the ground, the nice large grapes. I noticed they were somewhat shriveled. I thought they might not be good for eating, so I tasted a few to see if they were all right. They tasted sweeter than fully ripe grapes, so I kept picking and eating. I have some for you in the basket. Anyway, after a few minutes, I started getting this new feeling. My face lit up, getting warmer and warmer, and I began to feel happy."

Shela went toward the basket to look at the grapes. "They are the same kind of grapes we always eat. Just a little shriveled. Why would they make you feel different?"

"Maybe something happens to them, some sort of magic. I don't know. Try some."

She reached into the basket and began eating. After a few minutes, her face began contortions.

"You're right. I do feel different. Very happy.

This is great!"

For a few minutes, we looked at each other, both happy at what we had discovered, and happy because of how we felt.

"Maybe if I have more," I said, "I will be even happier."

I ate more grapes, and it was true; the more I ate, the happier I got. Soon the basket was empty. I stumbled down to the vines where the grapes grew--to pick more. I went back to the hut with my basket full. But this time, I ate only a few grapes and started getting dizzy. The hut was spinning around me. I fell asleep. The next morning, I felt strange. It was the opposite of the happiness from the day before. I was sick. When I touched my head, it throbbed. I wanted to go back to sleep. I felt pain everywhere. Shela said she felt the same way.

I don't understand how this could have happened.

But a few hours later, I felt fine. I began to

think again about how the grapes had made me feel so good. What kind of magic caused this strange happiness? I went back to the vines to see if I could discover their magic. At first, I picked some grapes that were normal, perfectly ripe. When I ate these, I did not get the feeling. But when I ate the shriveled grapes, after only a few minutes, I began to feel light-headed again.

I went back home to tell Shela about my discovery.

"Well," she said. "I don't want to eat grapes that make me feel sick the next day. We have children to feed. We forgot to feed the children yesterday because we were both so happy from those grapes."

"Well, fine," I said. "Do what you want. But this is a great discovery. I enjoyed being happy last night. It was the greatest feeling I have ever had. I intend to get it as often as I can. I'll probably become famous as the man who discovered shriveled grapes." She looked away, and I could tell she was not happy with my words.

Later that day, I got the idea of picking ripe grapes and putting them in the sun to shrivel. I thought that the magic might work better if I separated them from the vine where they could not grow. It worked. After a few days, I tried the grapes I had laid out, and got a most tremendous feeling. I spent that evening happy.

I noticed Shela looking at me strangely while I lay plastered by the fire. She asked me if I wanted to eat, and I told her I was too happy to eat.

The next day, I woke up with the bad feelings again. I knew they would go away soon, so I slept a little longer. Shela worked around the hut and fed the kids. Everything was fine when I awoke, except that she didn't say a word to me.

A few days later, I told my friend Herb about the shriveled grapes. We ate some and got happy together. He loved them more than I loved them. He staggered over to get our friend Biln who was our jingo partner. After Biln had eaten some grapes, he suggested we eat while we played jingo. We tried it, and laughed so hard we didn't notice who had won the game.

Herb came up with the idea to call our new feeling by a name. He said "happy" was too tame a word. He felt that "drunk" was a better word. We roared with laughter when he said it because the word rolled off his tongue in the silliest way.

"Druunnk," he said. We all said it, and it rolled off our tongues the same way. After our jingo game, we each stumbled home. This was the best jingo game we ever had!

On the way home, I stumbled into a neighbor's hut and knocked down a whole wall. When the neighbor saw it, he was very angry and told me I would have to fix it. He took me to the village elder and asked for a resolution. The village elder told me that I would have to fix the hut at my own expense. Now I have to spend a day not drinking so I can think straight and fix his hut. I'm sure Shela will be angry with me too. The village elder said that I should not drink and walk home at the same time. But it was only an accident and could have happened to anyone. I'll take my chances. It probably won't happen again. Besides, who are they to tell me how to live my life?

When I got home, I noticed that Shela was violently angry. She threw a pan at me after I walked through the door. I asked her what was wrong, and she said she had been working around the hut all day while I was getting happy. I told her that "drunk" was the correct word. Nevertheless, she said, she was doing my work while I was getting "drunk." She was not going to put up with it forever, she warned.

"Do what you want," I replied. "I am having fun. If getting drunk feels good, it is good to get drunk. A person should do what feels good. There is nothing you can do about it." The next day, after I got well, I went to see Herb. He was still in bed. Apparently, he had eaten more grapes than I. His wife, Alla, was very worried. She did not know that eating shriveled grapes had made him sick. So I did not tell her.

I went over to Biln's house to see if he wanted to eat some more grapes. He told me that he could not because he was working on a way to drink the grapes.

"That's a strange idea," I said. "It can't possibly work. Everyone knows you have to eat grapes."

"I am going to take ripe grapes and grind them up so they make a liquid. I'll put the liquid in a drinking vessel and cork it up. Then I'll leave it in the sun. We should be able to drink the grapes and still get drunk."

I thought it was a silly idea.

I staggered home that night and waited for Shela to throw a pan at me. This one caught me on the chin. I reacted with a feverish anger, picked up the pan and struck her on the head. That showed her who was boss. The kids woke up and started crying. Had it not been for their crying, I would have struck her again.

The next morning, she woke me up.

"When do you plan on getting back to normal life?" she asked.

"Why do you ask?" I said, rubbing my chin and my head.

"Well, there's a bump on my head. The children are afraid of you now. There is no meat for eating. The yard is a mess and hasn't been tended for weeks. The hut has a hole in the roof, and someone needs to fix it. Are we going to get back to a normal life?"

"Sure. Fix it yourself," I said. "I'll do what I want. Besides, you threw the pan at me. Tonight is my jingo night. I'll be home when I'm ready." I walked out of the hut.

I have never played jingo with a woman. But Herb brought a woman from the other village named Sonda. He had been telling her about our grapes and she was eager to try them. What a wild night! When we were all drunk, we laughed and told the loudest most raucous jokes. We even found a new way to play jingo. The loser had to remove an item of clothing. Sonda lost. Jingo is now more fun than ever.

Sonda and I got to liking each other. I could tell by the way she was looking at me. She said I was a great man because of my discovery. I don't remember getting home. I don't even know if Shela threw a pan at me. The first thing I remembered was that she and the kids were gone when I awoke. I went over to Herb's hut.

I found him and Sonda together in his bed. His wife was away for the weekend. Sonda thanked me for discovering the grapes. She felt privileged to have met a man who had made such a great discovery. She gave me that look again.

Biln came over with his first container of crushed grapes. We all drank it. Herb and Sonda liked the idea of drinking the grapes. Sonda seemed very impressed with Biln and started giving him the looks she had given me only a few moments before. She called him a great man. I was jealous that he thought of drinking the grapes first. Who does he think he is to improve on my discovery?
"Now we are getting drunk the right way." said Herb with a slurred voice. "We drank and

we are drunk." They laughed loudly.

I remember getting mad at Herb over Sonda. I became irritated when I saw her in his bed that day--but did not say anything until I was drunk. I had never argued with Herb before. I also got angry at Biln because he planned on selling his liquid grapes in the market plaza and Sonda now seemed to like him. He would get rich and I would not.

I guess being drunk makes you do things before you can stop yourself. I hit Herb with a drinking cup and opened his head. Sonda grabbed me fiercely by the hair and threw me out of the hut. I fell hard on my face, causing my nose to bleed. I didn't know she was that strong. Had I not been drunk, she could never have done it. So what, I didn't like her anyway. I'll find new drinking buddies.

The next day Biln took his drinking grapes to the market plaza. He told everyone that the liquid would make them happy. He sold all of it. That night many people came to his hut demanding more. He told them he was already preparing tomorrow's grapes. They threatened to kill him if he could not make more. Nevertheless, he was excited about the idea of selling his liquid grapes.

Shela and the kids left me. They moved back to her father's hut. A few days later, he came to talk to me.

"She says you are worthless. Since you discovered the grapes, you have done nothing but get drunk. You do not attend to her or the children. You shun your responsibilities and you blame her for this situation that is your fault. And worst of all, you beat and bully her. You are a drunk. I'm sorry for her because of what you have put her through. I am sad most for the children. They will have to grow up knowing their father is the world's first drunk. I hope they do not follow in your ways."

"But I am a great man," I said. "I'm the man who discovered shriveled grapes. I have given the world happiness. You do not appreciate my worth."

"You have violated nature's most important law. There is no greatness in that. You must understand that your mind is your most needed faculty. Your grapes destroy the mind. Many people have already discovered that and are wise enough to avoid the grapes. Don't you realize what you have lost?"

"My family?" I asked.

"You have lost that and much more: you have lost your soul. I hope you get it back someday. Until you do, good bye."

He walked out the door. I didn't worry about it. After all, my head was hurting. He had always tried to ruin my marriage. Now he had taken my family from me. It was his plan all along. My drinking had nothing to do with it.

These events happened several years ago. The world has changed greatly since my discovery. Men drink the juice when they eat, and they drink it during festivals. It makes every event merry. I have heard that our King drinks until he falls over dead drunk.

Herb and I never see each other. His wife left him when she found out about his drinking. But he stopped and she returned.

And he stopped seeing Sonda. She will now go with any man who has liquid grapes. But she won't associate with me because I know she's a drunk. I'm not afraid to tell her so. Biln is a rich man. He makes 500 gallons of liquid grapes a day and sells it for a high price. Men pay it. But he does not drink the grapes. Most of the women in our village hate him and spit in his path. He does not care.

There are many others selling the juice that is now called wine. And there are many getting drunk. If others do it, then it can't be bad. Biln tells people he discovered the shriveled grapes while picking fruit one day. Everyone believes him and he is hailed as a great man, the discoverer of shriveled grapes. I am known as the world's first drunk. I hate him. He is rich. I am poor. I know he is plotting against me.

Shela has married another man. He does not drink wine. I hate her for deserting me at the moment of my greatest triumph. I hate her for not eating shriveled grapes with me after that first night. That was her mistake in our marriage. People can be so cruel.

The medicine doctor says I will die soon. He says it is from drinking too much wine. I don't believe him and I refuse to stop drinking. What does a witch doctor know?

Last evening, I got violently sick when, for a laugh, some prankish boys served me water instead of wine. My body could not take the shock. So much for drinking buddies.

Everyone looks at me as if my life is a sad tale. They say it is terrible what too much wine can do to a man. But I say this, and will say it until my dying breath: No one...no one can tell you it is bad to have a good time. When you drink, you are happy and can do whatever you want. When you drink, you are a better person. Why should you stop? What's so bad about that? I don't care what they say. When I die, right thinking people, people like me, will say "Nobody told that man how to live."
As I lie here, I begin to remember what life was like before I made my great discovery. I suddenly remember how much I love Shela and my children. What if I had lived my life another way? I look around the room and wonder why everyone looks at me with

remorse. My children are lowering their heads. Where is my lovely Shela? I am trying to speak, but cannot. Why are you putting your hand over my eyes? I want to tell them that my life has been.......

Quiz on The World's First Drunk

The test below can be used as the foundation for group session discussions after the test. See the entire document below. You are free to print and use this document in group sessions as long as all links and copyright information is maintained.

Name _____

Date _____

1. What was this man's unspoken final thought? Can you finish his sentence? What do you think he was about to say? Here are some possibilities. You decide. Circle your answer/s
"I want to tell them that my life has been........"
- a wonderful experience.
- a waste.
- a life of accomplishment.
- lived according to my own principles.
- a rationalization.
- nothing but bad luck.

Your answer: _____

2. "Maybe if I have more, I will be even happier." Early in this person's use of alcohol, he discovered that the more he drank, the more drunk he became. This created a desire on his part to drink as much as possible. What was the result of this thought in his relationship with his wife?

_____

_____

_____

_____

_____

3. The first hangover. When he had his first hangover, his reaction was to notice when the pain ended and then he started thinking about getting drunk again. His wife, on the other hand, discovered the losses from this state and resolved to avoid it. What were those losses?

_____

_____

_____

_____

_____

4. "I intend to get it as often as I can." This is his decision after discovering the alcoholic state. At this point, a factor outside his control takes over his life. What is that factor?

_____

_____

_____

_____

5. "But it was only an accident and could have happened to anyone. I'll take my chances. It probably won't happen again." Taking chances on walking home drunk (or driving home today) is common among people who drink. Why is this a bad idea?

_____

_____

_____

_____

_____

_____

_____

_____

6. The first dysfunctional family. List the things that happened in this story that point to the breakdown of normal family relations.

_____

_____

_____

_____

_____

_____

_____

_____

7. Herb was the World's first drinking buddy. When two people drink large amounts of alcohol together, what can happen to their friendship?

_____

_____

_____

_____

_____

8. Moral choices: "I'll do what I want." This idea puts a person at odds with the responsibilities he/she has chosen and with the people to whom he/she has made commitments. What rationalizations (false justifications) would one have to think in order to allow him/herself to "do what I want?"

_____

_____

_____

_____

_____

_____

_____

_____

9. Doing things before you can stop yourself. Why couldn't this man control himself while he was drinking heavily?

_____

_____

_____

_____

_____

_____

_____

10. "...you blame her for this situation that is your fault." When a person must confront the problems drinking has caused, an easy thing to do is make up a "believable" rationalization. What were some of this man's rationalizations?

_____

_____

_____

_____

_____

_____

_____

_____

11. Nature's most important law. "You must understand that your mind is your most needed faculty." Why is this so? List examples and reasons why this is so.

_____

_____

_____

_____

_____

_____

_____

_____

12. How does excessive alcohol use violate "Nature's most important law?" List examples below.

_____

_____

_____

_____

_____

_____

_____

_____

13. "Having a good time." Alcohol often makes it possible to do things we cannot do while sober. We can feel happy, if we are not happy sober. We can be more forceful if we fear we are not forceful while sober. We can speak our mind, etc. "What's so bad about that?" In such cases a person comes to feel he really needs alcohol in order to live successfully. It becomes an integral part of his way of living. How can a person avoid getting into this situation?

_____

_____

_____

_____

_____

_____

_____

_____

1.   "But I am a great man," I said. "I'm the man who discovered shriveled grapes. I have given the world happiness. You do not appreciate my worth." Because the alcoholic has done great damage to his life and loved-ones, he tends to compensate by imagining himself to be a virtuous person who just happens to drink. This person develops a type of paranoia where he blames others for trying to harm him. What kinds of delusions have you found yourself engaged in?

_____

_____

_____

_____

_____

Notes:

Talking Points for a Group Leader

1. What was this man's unspoken final thought? Can you finish his sentence? What do you think he was about to say? Here are some possibilities. You decide. Circle your answer/s

"I want to tell them that my life has been........"

a wonderful experience.

a waste.

a life of accomplishment.

lived according to my own principles.

a rationalization.

nothing but bad luck.

There is no correct answer. Each individual's answer indicates where they are in their relationship with alcohol. In many cases, an individual will give the answer he/she thinks the group leader wants. The story is written in such a way, that the consequences of drinking are there, but enough of the hero's perspective is portrayed that many can sympathize or associate with him. Ask each individual what his/her answer is and ask why he/she chose that answer. Look for answers that will allow you to get a good dialogue going in the group.

2. "Maybe if I have more, I will be even happier." Early in this person's use of alcohol, he discovered that the more he drank, the more drunk he became. This created a desire on his part to drink as much as possible. What was the result of this thought in his relationship with his wife?

Suggestions:
-They disagreed about the importance and value of the discovery. This is called a value conflict. Value conflicts, if they are about important issues, can ruin marriages.
-It made her wonder about his character as a human being, something she had never wondered about before.
-At this point, they had a different outlook on the importance of raising children properly. He thought of alcohol and disregarded the children.
-They each interpreted problems from a very different perspective. For him, the only problem came when he was sober--and that problem was that he was not drunk. For her, the problem was his drinking and his

avoidance of his responsibilities. There are many others. Draw them out in discussion.

3. The first hangover. When he had his first hangover, his reaction was to notice when the pain ended and then start thinking about getting drunk. His wife, on the other hand, discovered the losses from this state and resolved to avoid it. What were those losses?

This point continues the discussion from question 2, except it relates to the value of drinking as such. She realizes that life must go on, things must be done. He believes that the only thing that must go on is drinking. What is a hangover? It is pain that results from the expulsion of alcohol or other drugs from the body. The subconscious mind, no longer anesthetized by the drug, attempts to regain its control over the nervous system. The result is pain and guilt. It happens because of the drug. Elicit as much discussion about this as possible. A hangover should be seen as a reason why drinking is dangerous for the mind and body because it has an effect on the mind's ability to recover its control over life.

4. "I intend to get it as often as I can." This is his decision after discovering the alcoholic state. At this point, a factor outside his control takes over his life. What is that factor?
Suggestions:
-Alcohol
-Drunkenness
-Avoidance of life's requirements

5. "But it was only an accident and could have happened to anyone. I'll take my chances. It probably won't happen again." Taking chances on walking home drunk (or driving home today) is common among people who drink. Why is this a bad idea?

This discussion is designed to point out, that even if a person drinks, because his judgment is impaired, he may still make a bad judgment to drink and drive. But the choice of drinking and driving can have negative consequences. And "taking a chance" actually makes the individual into a criminal who has violated the law. He is a criminal and this must be stressed. Oftentimes, an individual will make that choice to be a criminal under the premise that he/she will never be caught. Discuss why this is a crucial mistake.

Points of discussion:
• It is against the law
• It does make one a criminal---no matter what one thinks of oneself or how much one has contributed to the community in other ways.
• Accidents are more likely to happen while the individual is impaired
• There are legal and civil liabilities---jail, probation, possible job loss, legal bills and civil damages---that must be taken care of--- because of taking a chance on drinking and driving.
• Sooner or later something will happen.

6. The first dysfunctional family. List the things that happened in this story that point to the breakdown of normal family relations.

Suggestions:
-Value conflicts between man and wife
-Emotional disagreements
-Violence
-Psychologically harmed children
-Physical injury

-Possible legal and financial troubles

7. Herb was the World's first drinking buddy. When two people drink large amounts of alcohol together, what can happen to their friendship?

Suggestions:
-Uncontrollable disagreements
-Fights
-Loud conversation
-Blaming the world for each other's problems (rationalization)

8. Moral choices: "I'll do what I want." This idea puts a person at odds with the responsibilities he/she has chosen and with the people to whom he/she has made commitments. What rationalizations (false justifications) would one have to think in order to allow him/herself to "do what I want?"
Suggestions:
-It's my life
-No one can tell me what to do
-We are responsible for ourselves

-The world is full of do-gooders who want to tell others how to live

Discuss how a rationalization is only an excuse designed to avoid our involvement in a problem, a way of deflecting blame that most often is our own. Point out that a rationalization most often sounds reasonable. But it's purpose is to justify unreasonable actions.

9. Doing things before you can stop yourself. Why couldn't this man control himself while he was drinking heavily?

Suggestions:
-Alcohol intensifies emotions but reduces the ability to make sound judgments
-Alcohol impairs judgment so that when one decides to take action, one is not able to decide if the act is correct
10. "...you blame her for this situation that is your fault." When a person must confront the problems drinking has caused, an easy thing to do is make up a "believable" rationalization. What were some of this man's rationalizations?

Suggestions:
-She didn't drink with me. That was her mistake.
-She threw the pan at me
-She deserted me
-She is cruel

11. Nature's most important law. "You must understand that your mind is your most needed faculty." Why is this so? List examples and reasons why this is so.

Suggestions:
-Our mind makes important decisions
-We need a clear mind to decide correctly
-Our mind is our organ for thinking
-Clear thinking requires an unimpaired mind

12. How does excessive alcohol use violate "Nature's most important law?" List examples below.

Suggestions:
-Lowers reflex responses in our muscular system--this affects judgment
-Does damage to the brain and the entire body

-Thinking patterns used to rationalize behavior are used in other areas of one's life causing negative results in those areas

13. "Having a good time." Alcohol often makes it possible to do things we cannot do while sober. We can feel happy, if we are not happy sober. We can be more forceful if we fear we are not forceful enough while sober. We can speak our mind, etc. "What's so bad about that?" In such cases a person comes to feel he really needs alcohol in order to live successfully. It becomes an integral part of his way of living. How can a person avoid getting into this situation?

Suggestions:
-Get counseling
-Have non-drinking friends and support
-Take courses in areas where self-confidence suffers
-Confront the problem without aid from mind-altering substances
-Recognize the importance of dealing with issues and having psychological freedom without artificial substances

-Develop a value and goal-oriented approach to life that requires positive action rather than escape
-Learn to think about how you rationalize your behavior
-Recognize that you are either in control of your life or your life is out of control through your own choices--make the choice to control your life without any mind-altering substances

14. "But I am a great man," I said. "I'm the man who discovered shriveled grapes. I have given the world happiness. You do not appreciate my worth." Because the alcoholic has done great damage to his life and loved-ones, he tends to compensate by imagining himself to be a virtuous person who just happens to drink. This person develops a type of paranoia where he blames others for trying to harm him. What kinds of delusions would such a person think?

Accomplishments, real or imagined, cannot cover the fact that one is doing damage to oneself and others, especially family members when one drinks heavily.

Possible examples:
- They hate me
- They are trying to get me
- My wife doesn't appreciate my value
- My wife is trying to put my children between us
- I am a great man
- I have accomplished great things

Group Leader's notes on open discussion:

Alcoholism and Addiction – the System

These four books comprise a system that can be used by both patients and counselors who are battling Alcoholism and Addiction. Based upon Mr. Villegas's own system developed during his struggle against alcoholism, this system includes:

Alcoholism and Addiction – A Secular Ten-Step Program

This groundbreaking book offers a secular approach to alcoholism unlike that offered by Alcoholics Anonymous. We recommend that every individual going for alcohol and drug-abuse counseling be given a copy of this book which contains the workbook and the two versions of The World's first drunk. http://amzn.to/2md6R9w $3.45 Kindle $11.95 softcover

The Secular Ten-Step Program Workbook

This booklet covers the program developed by Mr. Villegas. It is designed as a workbook with blank spaces for the patient to write his own thoughts as he takes each of the ten steps. Order one copy for each patient in counseling. http://amzn.to/2lrHimS $4.49 Kindle $6.95 softcover

The World's First Drunk – With Counselor Talking Points

This booklet is designed for the counselor as he works with patients during individual or group therapy. It contains helpful tips on discussing the life story of the man who invented alcohol. Order one copy for each patient in counseling. http://amzn.to/2l446Wr $2.99 Kindle $5.95 softcover

The World's First Drunk – Patient Version

This version of the short story contains empty spaces where the patient can answer questions about the life story of the man who invented alcohol. Order one copy for each counselor. http://amzn.to/2ldxBGb $2.99 Kindle $5.95 softcover.

www.robertvillegas.com

www.ingramcontent.com/pod-product-compliance
Lightning Source LLC
Chambersburg PA
CBHW070132290526
45789CB00005B/2207